Former Latin teacher and keen amateur chef James M'Kay has been writing and performing his poems, as well as devising and running events to perform them at, since the year 2000.

Having helped to launch a number of poetic careers from his DIY cabaret night *Home Cooking* in Newcastle, he moved to London in 2005, where he became involved with Richard Tyrone Jones' influential *Utter! Spoken Word* project. He now lives at Gravesend in Kent, where he is the host of monthly neighbourhood poetry night *Reverb Chamber*.

Very Friendly Weapon is James' second published collection of poems, the first being *Quiet Circus* (Vintage Poison Press, 2011). He also appears on the poetry-and-prog-rock album *Follow On* by Newcastle band The Morris Quinlan Experience (Round and Round Records, 2007), which gained national and international airplay and led to a live performance at London's much-missed 12 Bar.

Very Friendly Weapon

James M'Kay

Burning Eye

BurningEyeBooks
Never Knowingly
Mainstream

Copyright © 2018 James M'Kay

The author asserts the moral right under the Copyright, Designs and Patents Act 1988 to be identified as the author of this work.

All rights reserved. No part of this publication may be reproduced, stored in a retrieval system, or transmitted, in any form or by any means without the prior written consent of the author, nor be otherwise circulated in any form of binding or cover other than that in which it is published and without a similar condition being imposed on the subsequent purchaser.

This edition published by Burning Eye Books 2018

www.burningeye.co.uk

@burningeyebooks

Burning Eye Books
15 West Hill, Portishead, BS20 6LG

ISBN 978-1-911570-35-6

Very Friendly Weapon

CONTENTS

Graffiti Tourism	8
I Want to Be a Penguin Modern European Poet	9
Lines from a Glasgow Cemetery	10
On Dreams	11
North Is a State of Mind	12
Odes One Four	13
Roman Hexameters	14
Good Friday	16
Speechless	17
Dollywood in the Rain	18
Lea Bridge Road	19
Midsummer Night, Travelling North	20
Sound Guy for the Sirens	22
Circumnavigator	23
There'll Always Be	24
Sleeping in Summer	25
Three Hundred Thousand	26
Song for Uranus	29
I Bear Witness	32
Through a White Cloud/ Waiting at Arrivals	33
Banshee	34
Hangover Psalm	35
Piccadilly	36

Ikaros	37
Bench	38
One Last Night in Paris	39
Empty Sutra	40
Buoyancy	41
Not Far from Here	42
Don't Look	43
We Are Grandbabies	44
In These Sinking Lands	46
Rapture	47
Gravesend, Extraction	48
The Land Is Bright	49
Odes One Eleven	52
After a Couplet of Rochester	53
The Day Before the Calendar Ran Out	54
Faggot Hexameters	56
Two Lines from Homer	58
We Are Posterity	59
Tantalos	60
Brave New Year/Happy New World	61

GRAFFITI TOURISM

It is written:
stones shall grow petals,
bricks shall have eyes,
fish swim on concrete,
streets bleed rainbows,
words sprout like weeds
and the city shall speak.

Make wide the meeting place
and smooth the dancing floor!
The snake is shot,
the water drinkable again!

One by one my previous
desires return to me.
In dreams I meet my younger,
skinnier self slumped and basking
in the shallows of a house party,
Nina Simone playing live
on the meat-room piano.
Nice party – nice dream,
woke up stiff as a board…

All the birds are screaming,
all the clouds are gone
and the writing on the wall says:
POETS SHIT FLOWERS.

I WANT TO BE A PENGUIN MODERN EUROPEAN POET

I want to be a Penguin Modern European Poet.
I will wear a communist suit with dissident spectacles.
I will write in a language that looks suitably attractive
and undecipherable;
my name will be genuinely difficult to pronounce
instead of being just easy to pronounce wrong.

On my slim volume, impeccably modernist,
tightly bound and violently designed,
the negative of my face, double exposed
in acid colours that shine like a Day-Glo star.

I want to be discovered, bright and ageless,
in the dusty back room of a bookshop.
I want to be read late at night,
a few lines at a time, by one who hasn't
properly realised yet that cigarettes really
are bad for you and coffee is best
kept for mornings.

I will write dangerous ideas
and They (and everybody else)
will think it's just about tractors.

LINES FROM A GLASGOW CEMETERY

and my basket is empty
and my basket runs over like a wilderness
inside the lone voice of a prophet

             Keith Jarrett

You're right, Keith. It has everything to do
with wilderness, with fullness and of course
with empty. Love is having first of all
enough to eat; wisdom and song start with
escaping from the fullness of the nations,
the belly and the head. How shall the voice
be heard where other voices throng? Where will
it sound if not in the cathedral of
a hollow, thoughtless mind? Which is to say
that without wasteland there can be no truth:
where everything is full, there is no music.

ON DREAMS

Stage-moon on a wire.

Stone-dark, the sea made of
fine, powdered glass.

Death and Sleep,
twin angels and a certain
fabulous light.

I awake from
yet another dream of singing
'Newham Town Hall' to the tune of
'Mull of Kintyre'.

And again,
the rest of the lyric
escapes me.

NORTH IS A STATE OF MIND

Outside it is a region stretched too much, the empty page
beneath the map always almost showing through.

It is an exquisite melancholy, boredom mainly with occasional
flares of temper, wild dreams and wide, blank landscapes.

The smell of coal fires along the old terraces.
Silence in big white flakes, only the wind alive and curious:

what grows grows quick and headstrong, before the rain.
In this degree of emptiness, everyone's a hero or no one is.

Are there dragons here? Painted ones, ghosts, and less than
    ghosts:
names. Farmers Arms. Son of Timeslip. Handyside Arcade.

The dregs of the day shine the apples on a streetcart.
The city's night haze begins to turn the low cloud lilac.

They rebranded the bus station an *interchange*, meaning
nothing begins or ends here these days, just passes through.

The road north and the road south are one road and the same.
Leaving home is harder, and takes longer, than you think.

ODES ONE FOUR

from the Latin of Horace

Bitter winter vice case
solved gratifyingly.
Machines haul out
boats too long dry.
Frost whitens not
one pasture more.

Dance with grace and decency,
the moon impends! Volcanoes
dark in the basement
fire up the boilers! Liberated earths
bear flowers for your hair!

Pale death knocks on all doors,
blessed comrade.
Life's short running time allows
no long game.
Soon comes a night with no drinking,
no bingo
and no up-and-coming Lycidas to ogle
while his looks last.

ROMAN HEXAMETERS

for Giuseppe Gioachino Belli (1791–1863)
and Arthur Hugh Clough (1819–1861)

Well, Uncle Gigi, I sit in your bar by the Casa di Dante,
watching your people enjoy their Sunday afternoon coffee.
I have had too much coffee already today, but I summon
yet more *espresso* to get my mind racing down unfamiliar
roads – hexameters, if you please! – this new-found thing for
regular metre perplexes me, schooled as I am in only the
freest of free verse – anyway, shouldn't it really be sonnets?

Rome disappoints me much, wrote the minor Victorian poet,
proving that to the dull all things are, predictably, dull – the
cool spring breeze through the window is throwing the menus
down on the floor, setting the waitresses running to put them
back again – Rome disappoints me hardly at all; on the contrary,
Rome is more dreamlike than dreams themselves. The Tiber is swollen,
bursting its banks; my usual spot for a smoke and a quiet
loiter is quite submerged, and I wander from café to café,
aimless. What was I thinking to leave my book in the hotel
room this morning? But, then again, what need of a book here?

Look, in a little piazza a tail-coated cellist rehearses a Bach suite,
milking the *tempi* in the Italian way, which produces
music more for the bedroom than for the mind, or the dancefloor;
yet his long supple cadences tail me down cobbled alleys,
wind themselves into the wandering smells of lunch from the kitchens,
ring like bells in the light on the fountains, the rust and the festooned
sun-bathing laundry. Brings me up short, back to the cold, grey,
wet archipelago over the mountains: there on the corner,
outside the kiosk, news of the death of the *lady di ferro*.

Memory surges: that day at the end of the cold, grey eighties;
stout comrade Hemingway posted outside the exam room to
 tell me,
'Thatcher is gone!' We rampaged the halls, chanting,
 'SOLIDARNOSC!
SOLIDARNOSC!' But that was a different century; others
just as bad, if not worse, have taken her place since. Comrades,
hold the champagne, save our dancing for victory; let the world
 turn, her
poor old body be nothing, her name completely forgotten.

GOOD FRIDAY

Hampton Court, a garish, drunk
and sunburned London scene.
Cock-happy little Tarzans
rampage about in hire-boats.
Disinterest of the womenfolk.
Disdain and jollification combine
in the riverside beer gardens.

Behind old brick walls, cool air,
liquid with horticulture.
I chew a bunch of beech leaves:
flesh dissolves first,
the veins a moment after.
Young ones, the slightest,
purest taste of green.

SPEECHLESS

Came upon a flower and it was spring
by a less-frequented path and
better than all birthdays.

There is a place where
sighs stand for sentences
and tongues are only good
for warm, wet fingers.

Further on, much further, is a hilltop
crowned with gold, deep-set with pinks,
and daisies trace our path like stars
or spilt milk beneath the pines.

Came upon a meadow in the full of summer,
heady and exhausted and the blousy senses
droop, and the dancing hive sends ever
back and forth her honeybees
to feed the dark that translates
even fading beauty into sweetness
against the dead times.

DOLLYWOOD IN THE RAIN

First of all,
the mountains are beautiful
and sing with waterfalls.

As elsewhere, people talk, eat,
cry out, stand, look
and move on, spending money.
You never saw
such a big frying pan.

You never screamed so hard,
laughing and at every corner,
round every turn, that music
alive with the sound of the hills again.

My camera failed twice.

Once: the fierce little blur there is
the blessed mother of the precinct herself,
you're just going to have to believe me.

And once again, more philosophically:
if you could photograph love,
there'd be no call for poets.

LEA BRIDGE ROAD

Sun makes gold like fireworks
the thunder-shower aftershock
beneath the dripping chestnut tree.

We should be flat on our backs.

MIDSUMMER NIGHT, TRAVELLING NORTH

Sardined, sandwiched and shot
from King's Cross' smoky muzzle north
on the tail of the slow-dying day.

Goodbye was a smile in a doorway.
'Are you really so happy,'
I wanted to ask, 'or is it just
professionalism?'

Alexandra Palace, the tunnels
and the suburbs, Stevenage,
Peterborough – somewhere round here
my grandfather fell dead from the sleeper
1931, leaving his body for morning to find.

Stevenage, Peterborough,
the suits and the secretaries,
his name on all her papers,
quick drink after, then heads down
for supper, the sofa and the screen.

In the sudden emptiness
the old sprawl (what memory there is
in posture!) returns from years past,
coming down, coming home,
pockets full of flyers,
bills from cafés, dope, comic books
and general *dolce vita*.

Doncaster, halfway and as usual
the ghost of a hard-on.

Towards York the horizon grows
faint and thick with hills.
Somewhere far away autumn is born.

In the true north they are saying
nothing (what dreams there are

in half-light, in half-sleep!), staying secret
in wide meadows
with many silent others,
picking nine kinds of flowers?
Seven kinds of flowers?
And there's the charm.

Darlington, Durham,
the digger factory and the grand
curve of Newcastle Central Station.
Canyons of glass, rivers of cars,
the rough wind cold against
the women's thighs,
nameless stains on the pavement.

Shell sand, sugar sand,
strung out with beach fires
into the summer dim
into the distance.

SOUND GUY FOR THE SIRENS

White rocks white sun white sea
white sand white noise
the constant sound of knitting
as the crabs with legs like needles pick
through half-sunk skeletons,
the waves on all those bones.

Dead fans mostly. The occasional
Nereid stunned by the sub-bass
and washed ashore to vibrate
and decay with the rest of them.

Not that I ever felt that leaping-over-
the-side-to-a-watery-grave effect
the critics raved about. It's having seen
themselves backstage, I shouldn't wonder.

We on the technical side were always
keener on our never-ending weekends
over at the Lotus Eaters', and our trips
to Circe for a bit of the animal stuff.

White rocks white sun white sea
white sand white noise gaffer tape
cold coffee overflowing ashtrays,
immortal as anything ever is.

CIRCUMNAVIGATOR

Glory be to God for kerosene,
the reflectivity of metal and
the singing of tormented air! Heathrow –
arriving on a bright spring evening, hours
to go until a cheap hotel room and
a job to start at dawn, I set myself
to walk around the blank periphery.

Corralled between high banks of razor wire,
nobody else on foot, continuously
above me to the left the concrete and
grass ramparts of the shabby international
freight town, the tin and plastic cabins of
the global things-and-money racket. On
the right a tawdry hedgeland prospect, clumps
of scrub the only feature in a scraggy tract
of grass and waste flowers. Somewhere a blackbird sings.
Nobody else on foot, but faces stare
through windscreens, angry and incomprehending.

I shout out every poem I can think of,
throat open like a turbine duct until
I don't know what I'm howling any more.
The jets ascend into the crimson sun,
a string of diamonds thundering in behind.

Wind and the sun's low rays wrench soft tears from
my struggling face. The words follow the planes
up out across the world away from here,
this city that is not a city and
this road nobody needs to walk.

THERE'LL ALWAYS BE

It is this we learn, tripping startled
into the blank heart of the long weekend:
gravity ain't all that.

Good enough music could put us into orbit,
but hadn't we better get our heads around the
bottom of the garden first?

Cut-price soothsayers slouch by the bonfire
and the sleeping chickens.
Night is unmysterious as day,
darker in places, different things to buy:
pockets of brokenness, sofas of sand,
sofas of sand.

Things which are – hedges, glitter,
romantic comedy – are, whether anyone
believes in them or not.
You'll know it when you bite into it.
Is there honey still? Lick your tired smile:
a little salt soon brings out the sweet.

Nearing the brink the torrents quicken.
Minutes drop like ripe fruit behind
summer foliage. Nothing is ours to save,
but this is not over. If a thing's worth doing,
it's worth doing again. The earth smiles beneath
us. Soon will come butterflies.

SLEEPING IN SUMMER

Sleeping in summer is the real thing.
In winter it's too easy, the lesser of two evils
in an unwelcoming world.

But when the night air is sweet and warm,
and the night itself beautiful and brief
that the city does not stop for,
nor the creatures of the field,
sleep is greatest of pleasures.

Naked in a room,
a single sheet for propriety's sake,
or blissed out at last in the tall grass
till roused by fear of the strengthening
sun on your white legs.

THREE HUNDRED THOUSAND

The last time I saw Jimmy Savile – wait,
the first time I saw Jimmy Savile – hang on,
the only time I ever saw Jimmy
Savile – it was the morning of the day
the sky fell in and he was running, quarry-like,
hard on his tail the first of the shambolic
horde that fell on Roundhay Park that day.

From concrete towers and blank estates, from towns
that sleep their rusted post-industrial sleep
beside the grey-green hills, forgotten rivers,
silent factories and silver seas,
their hollow faces burning – ecstasy
for breakfast on a weekend like no other! –
they staggered in their thousands. Friends, this was
the Radio 1 Love Parade in Leeds,
AD two thousand.
                            'Jimmy fucking Savile!'
Unsteady arms reached out in wonder, smiles
of children smiled again round speed-fucked teeth,
and no way past the stumbling embrace
and protestations of 'I love you, man!'
A garish rabbit in the headlights of
the juggernaut he started forty years
before to get his hands up teenage skirts,
bewildered and alone, he turned and ran.

And he was not the only one to get
it wrong that day. The metropolitans
who planned this thing to hit their regional
programming targets (bringing urban chic
to the benighted provinces) were not
to know that in those days flights to Berlin
were cheaper than the train to London, weren't
to know how empty cities sang from north
to north, machines of loving grace beneath
brick arches, concrete under derelict skies,

were not to know that what to them was fashion
was here a broad church with a congregation
undreamed of in their Soho bar philosophies.
In short, they planned for thirty thousand and
three hundred thousand came.

The phones went first. Not that we'd had them long,
but long enough to wander off from friends
safe in the knowledge they'd be findable
again. They weren't. The soft rain hardened. On
the grassy banks we strained to hear the music.
The massed and jostling regiments besieged
the stage, desperate to drown in waves of bass,
but only trickles made it through the press
of flesh and barely moistened. Anyone
with anything to drop dropped like a stone.
Whole legions of the disconnected lay
in piled heaps, others roamed about like zombies,
and all the thousand various shades of brown
and pink and grey twatted, bollocksed monkeys
cavorted angrily about. And now
the light came down like something out of Shakespeare:
I know a bank where the wild thyme blows,
Where oxlips and the nodding violet grows,
Quite over-canopied with luscious woodbine,
With sweet musk-roses and with eglantine.
I swear I had no drugs that day.

Somewhere beyond the Yorkshire cloud the sun-
machine was coming down. Against all odds
one scattered tribe regathered, falling back
to where a pasty-seller'd smuggled in
unsanctioned decks behind his van. And then
at last we danced. Bodies of noise, bodies
of zero dissatisfaction, driving our feet
up to the ankles in the mud and heads
full under the Aphex Twin and basically

the body is articulated meat,
a puppet in the war of friction, legs
and gravity, a flailing toy strung through
with noise…

Retreating, over the ensuing hours
and days, the horde flooded the station road
with sprawling knots of barely sentient carnage,
humanity like lichen, lounging and spaced,
and mitsubishi'd all before them, gouging
homeward trails of devastation. Days
elapsed before the last casualties cleared
the wards of hospitals for miles around.
Glass carpeted sharply the grassy banks
for weeks. The sky came down. Our shoulders and
our shoes got slowly damp and we just let it happen.
Shimmer turned to afterglow and ebb
and flow and beautiful and lost always.

SONG FOR URANUS

for Richard Tyrone Jones

Eight minutes is a long time for a poem, however you count it.
Best to begin setting out my stall – tell them what you're about to
tell them, tell them it, then tell them what you've just told them –
or, as Aristotle puts it, beginning, middle, and end. So,
asked to contribute a poem on an astronomical theme, I
instantly think of Manilius, dullest of all ancient poets,
whose *Astronomica* I have frankly not read, but reminds me
such didactic endeavours fit best in dactylic hexameters.
Much the best metre for exposition, tending in English
towards the chatty and heterogeneous (quiet in the cheap seats!);
bouncing along, they render the educational painless.

So far, so good. With the form sorted, let us proceed to the content:
here lies the rub. Though this science-and-poetry crossover thing is
all very Zeitgeist, it all too often results in a sort of
bum Wikipedia in verse, rehearsing a whole load of numbers:
so many gases comprise the atmosphere; it takes so long
to orbit the Sun, so long to turn on its axis; the number and
names of its satellites are as follows… Equations are more use,
comrades, for this sort of thing, and more beautiful, too – who needs poems?

I think, though, I might just have found what is called, in the business, an angle.
Scientists beware! Classicists-stroke-queertheoryheads can be just as
geeky as anyone wearing a lab coat. Head full of books is
head full of books, for all that. And so I entitle my talk *While
Men Are from Mars and Women from Venus, Gays Come from*
– and no, I
won't, Richard, be inveigled into pronouncing the name the

way it sounds like I'm angling for cheap laughs – God forbid in this
dizzying intellectual environment anyone angling for
cheap laughs! – this is rich meat indeed, and we're to have plenty.

Uranus is my song, and begins with the eye and its nakedness.
Long time ago, when they first started taking note of the slowly
wheeling skies of the dark hours, they saw that most of the lights up
there remain in fixed constellation each with the others, but
seven did not, and these they called *planets* – 'wanderers' – and the
empty space in between, that floods diurnally blue at the
glance of the jealous sun and drowns out the rest, they called
Ouranos – 'heaven' – the eternal and featureless up. To their way of
thinking, these seven variables on a rotating field said
all that needs to be said about life in all of its diverse
ramifications, revealing the workings of Fate like a clockwork
toy. Nowadays we like to make fun of emperors who wouldn't
go for a shit before taking astrological readings,
we're so rational these days, so much more advanced – or we think so.

Meanwhile, lacking a star of their own, some looked to the void for
patronage. Plato, describing the tortuous road between pleasures that
leads from the glimpse of a beautiful boy to that final solution
where the philosopher's soul rejoins the Light it first sprang from,
called it *Uranian* – 'heavenly' – love, to set it outside the
expectations and sublunar norms of the ordinary people.

Cut to centuries later. Machines were unveiling new worlds, new
kinds of human began to emerge, needing new kinds of label.

Some sat up late in the gas-lit night with coffee and pipe-
    smoke,
conning their Plato, and made a first stab: not yet *homosexuals*,
not even *inverts*, their word for themselves (and for us) was
    Uranian.
Carpenter, Hirschfeld, all you dead heroes, who thought of
    yourselves as
born between genders and therefore free as the sky!
    Transcending is
easy for those with the right education and leisure to wander.
Heroes, though.
                        But when the eye lost its nakedness,
innocence followed.
Clothing itself to enter a dark, cold, distant domain, it became
    too
difficult not to apply new techniques to the science of the self.
    If the former
name for the vast empty sky was reassigned to a lump of
orbiting matter, the love that had been transcendent desire and
pursuit of the whole is now just a hypothetical gene that
nobody's even bothered to claim to have found yet. Pace the
LGBTNP, no human is born anyhow except
naked and screaming. Hypothetical genes are no realer than
Shelley von Strunckel's column tonight in the *Evening Pravda* –
should have said *Standard*, sorry – wandering just a bit far from
the brief, do you reckon? Did you not realise planets are tools
    for
thinking with? And the colder the planet, the stranger the
    thought? These
rambling unscientific hexameters do seem to suit a
rambling and unscientific kind of a song, which is fine till you
want to draw to a close. My song, I guess, therefore my
    problem.
What does Aristotle say? Beginning, middle and end, or
tell them what you're going to tell them, tell them it, and then
tell them what you've just told them. This sums it up, I think,
    nicely:
this is for all the stars and the planets. I love you all.

I BEAR WITNESS

When they threw me from the building
the world warped and stretched like toffee.

When they threw me from the building
I fell like Alice with wind in my skirts
to land in wonder. When they threw
me from the building I grew wings.

When they threw me from the building
the air in my ears roared deafening angelic harmonies.

When they threw me from the building
it wasn't nearly so high as I thought,
little more than a kerbstone.
'All depth is a trick of perspective,'
I concluded cheerfully, picked
myself up and walked away.

When they threw me from the building
I landed on my feet, I caught the bus,
got caught in the rain but made it to the party.

My eye betrayed me and I did not pluck it out.
My hand betrayed me and I did not strike it off.
When they threw me from the building
it was all of me that landed.
When they threw me from the building
I was freer than they were.
When they threw me from the building
my first cry and my last was LOVE.

THROUGH A WHITE CLOUD

WAITING AT ARRIVALS

Ivy hanging

off the garage

waves

like a curtain,

tendrils curled

around the old cinder block

in horizontal

rain.

Caleb Beissert
Asheville, North Carolina

                    Tourists surging

                through the gate in

                        waves.

            The concrete path

                    remembers

the burning heat of the day.

            Last night I dreamed of

                        clouds.

James M'Kay
Dalaman, Turkey

BANSHEE

Always a bar scene,
always some chanteuse
(may not be cheap
but professional enough to look it)
opens with a rush
like a hit of rough wine.

Rhythm, exhaustion,
everyday sainthood.
It is a poor life
that does not know tiredness
but the music is good,
the ministers of drunkenness
many-coloured and beguiling
and the drinking is easy.

You keep on losing your voice
and you keep on finding it again,
more battered and more useful
every time.

You ask yourself,
*How many virginities
are there still left to lose?*
and the answer comes,
YES.

HANGOVER PSALM

or 'States of Bodily Discomfort Can Sometimes Be Alleviated by Pretending to Be Allen Ginsberg'

Holy! Holy! Holy!
The drinking of poisons is holy!
The regurgitation of residues is holy!
Drought is holy!
Thirst is holy!
Stickiness is holy!

The surplus daylight of the morning is holy!
Holy the neon red veins deep in the eyeball!
Holy the cruel racket of the feathered species!
Holy siege engines assail the poor earholes!

The penitential neck is holy!
Holy the grip of spiritual pliers!
The suffering brow is holy!
Holy the pinch of the invisible vice!

Sackcloth of bright traffic!
Holy remorse!
Ashes of memory!
Scourges of cold sweat!

Blessed is the cup of quiet tea.
Blessed are the small white tablets.

Holy the uncertainty of step!
Holy the belongings left behind as sacrifice on trains!
Blessed the embrace of fresh pillows
and blessed are the poems that come
when you're too busy feeling
sorry for yourself to stop them.

PICCADILLY

Killing dusktime
leant against a Piccadilly shopface with
Sir Walter Scott and cool, strong saleslight
shifting the page a stroboscopic pane
of churchglass under the deathless doggerel.

Accosts me in passing
and a high-functioning Polish accent
a young moustache, giggles with his girlfriend
to find one reading a book
here, these crazy fucking English
(and I'm not even all English).

IKAROS

… and you can call me anything you want,
he said. OK, maybe I call you Ikaros
descended among coffee chains and gum-
blossom, not the sea you were expecting.

… and no rest is ever final. As the slabs
that pave London fade and vanish
under the weight of your god-weary gaze,
we find you breaking fall a moment
to rest your wax and feather scars here among
cobblestones, church spires and piss stains.

… and no fall is ever finished. Already in some
sunny elsewhere leaves and vines, bells and bright
sun languages reach out spreading to catch you.

Meteor flying, falling; no matter.
You know you could always fly.
Don't know why you thought you ever
needed wings.

BENCH

Rained kisses pucker the canal all over.
He presses into him, the soft push of
a kitten's head. Friends synchronising crises.

'Whatever changes me is part of me,'
one says – or starts to say, or thinks of saying;
it's really not important in a scene
where speaking sank into telepathy
some time back – and the other says, or tries
to say, or thinks of saying, 'Isn't it, though?'

Five crows sit on a wet branch. Time to go
and kiss goodbye to walls which have contained us
happy, through rainier afternoons than this.

ONE LAST NIGHT IN PARIS

It's a poem if I say it is.

Trapped in this sleep machine
behind immovable glass when the
mercy the streets have been praying for
finally hits Paris, the lit windows
in the apartment skyline blur,
a delicate change in the background hum,
or else you'd never know.

Pull on clothes, wait for elevators,
brave the lobby conference guests
and tour groups to finally gulp air
in the dry patch by the car park entrance.

Headlights! Headlights! Rain!
Headlights! Rain!
Spouting poems out loud like a nutcase!
Headlights! Rain!

EMPTY SUTRA

for Mike Cook (d. 2013)

September twenty twelve, a mountain town.

The suffocating summer heat is gone
but lives again under the stage lights where
these poets strut and sweat and soar. Of whom
one noble soul, more wasted even than
is customary at these functions, stumbles
to find the mic, opens his drunken throat,
evacuates the weariness inside him.

'Empty!' he roars, and over and again
'Empty! Empty!' until he empties out
the syllables themselves of all significance.

Backstage we stare with wide eyes at the clock.
Outside, along the kerb, leaves flee the wind.
A pretty mouth moves loudly in a face
of redneck whiskers, nothing more. Empty.

I drank with him a few times, shared a stage
or two. Before a year had passed he upped
and killed himself is all I know, and be
the low road gentle on his pilgrim feet.

BUOYANCY

Everyone grows ever lighter,
some gradually, some of a sudden
or slowly or by fits and starts:
to live is to lose mass.
Footprints all grow shallower
until one day they float free of the planet,
losing patience with restraint.

Of those around us
first we lose the neck and shoulders,
then the breasts, hands and fingers,
knees and ankles until finally
the feet slip up and out of reach,
as the escaping fish flicks her tail.

Looking up we see the endless series
of human generation rising into space,
smaller and smaller to a perfect net
of tiny lights in the darkening east,
each rank each rank stretching always up
to touch again the nearest departed.

Looking up we wonder
what they do up there out of reach
but always in sight of each other.

Looking down we marvel
how those pale tendrils of yesterday
are grown to loving branches that cling
to our necks our shoulders breasts hands fingers
ankles and will one day have to let go entirely.

NOT FAR FROM HERE

Not far from here
the hours lose their scent
and the trails are fading.
What footprints there
are are no two of a kind
or common direction.
Are those stars, or just tiny
rips in the canvas?
The image always
threatens to resolve…

To protect my peace of mind
I spend a lot of time
dropping stones into dark water.
I know what's reflected.
I don't need to see it,
sweet enough the songs
turbulence sings to itself.

And sometimes you go out
to get drunk or get laid
or hear poems or whatever
for what seems like the millionth time
and it ends up bells and thunder
out of nowhere feeling like
the first all over again.

DON'T LOOK

Small berries in red bunches
(red as the raincoat of a dead child
or murderous dwarf) beneath
canal-water skies stand out
like clusters of obscene Braille
on the townscape's paper skin.

The tearing of enormous paper
is one of the sounds that suggests itself
in the always-present swell and murmur,
growl and purr of traffic.

On a clear day you can see
right across to the bypass.

On a clear day the bypass also
sees right across to you.

WE ARE GRANDBABIES

Young and hungry I supposed being a poet
to consist urgently in garrets and coffee shops
drafting and issuing fiery manifestos.

Having since eaten rather well I seem to have
managed these several years without
having written a single one, until…

It is to be immeasurably deep, naked and kind.

First of all kind to the ladiesandgentlemen;
it is their evening too. Then deep,
long in the roots, tooth-strong,
naked in an emperor's junk-shop
suit of vintage empty (overempty streetside,
underempty next the skin), and deep,
which from another point of view is high.

Kind, for what seems childish now .
may yet turn out to have been
most grown-up all along, and kind
to all the people just trying to make a living;
they are naked too.
Actors wear costumes, poets
supply our own nakedness.
Book the right floor show,
every house is a bawdy house.

Deep down to the empty gut and laughs.
Naked and unafraid. Deep and rising.
Kind and quite prepared to look like an idiot.

It sees a spade and naked it says *spade*,
a poet and says *poet*. It knows less respectable
four-letter words than that, but kind is
often to speak gentlier.

Deep we are few, kind we are many,
and all of us naked grandbaby poets
and we speak beautifully each to another.

Kind to sisters and brothers of all tribes,
even if they don't think yet that
Howl and Other Poems is the best book ever.

Deep because this is no desk job.

And kind in the end to yourself,
that whatever your burden sit lightly,
your work-songs be taken for skylarking
and victory.

IN THESE SINKING LANDS

Capital and cities throw up corpses, heaps of them.
Light to liquid, weight into rolling waves.
Certain things flow: coffee, semen, rain, glass.

That absinthe hour just keeps on approaching.
Another day, another addiction.
Jack, escalation isn't progress.

Crotch hair curling fire, black as a raven.
Beautiful and drunk on every square in Europe.
All the latest features and no off button.

All constellations are temporary.
Only a few wanderers are constant.
One clear day I will look for you.

RAPTURE

All my bodily fluids
turn to beautiful insects.

I spit; it has butterfly wings,
flickers off through the
open night window.

My eyes leak rainbow
centipedes in sinuous lines.

Iridescent foam of tiny beetles
surges from the used tissue
drift by the bed.

I bare my wrists,
blade ready, knowing
my blood will emerge
all at once
a great crimson moth
and wrap its translucent self
several times
about the bare lightbulb.

In the red, red room
a jilted papery husk
settles lightly down
on a rented carpet.

GRAVESEND, EXTRACTION

This was always a transit town.
The arrivals and departures industry,
wrenchings away with hopes
and forebodings of returns
and forgetfulness.

Always one more one last night before
the fission of the dawn, from which
one escapes into the big wide world
and the other carries a sad
piece of it home with him.

Meanwhile on planet Novocain
there is struggle but no pain.
Tooth rot, mouth rot, anger too
can be extracted from a heart
numbed against all ache.
So good it almost makes you forget
where's the cleanest place of all…

The children behind me
on the bus home are brainstorming
names for the nightclub
they're planning to open
in the empty shop
that used to be the Blockbuster.
There's a hole in my head
lined with clotted velvet,
black to the eye, red to the tongue.

'What kind of music are we going to have?'
'Anything, whatever Johnny plays.'

Johnny is their friend
who's going to DJ.

THE LAND IS BRIGHT

Friends, Romans,
fellow travellers,
lend me your eyes:
the land is bright.

The old bars, the old faces,
the old days nearly all gone now.
The people are dark but
the land is bright.

You come round early morning
on a late-night sofa and your pants
are surprisingly not round your ankles.
There is at least one gentleman still,
the land is bright.

On inspection, all you have
to show for it is the slightly roached
business card of an actress
you don't remember meeting,
the land is bright.

Until finally you realise
all over again that it's
yesterday's survival tactics
fuck you up today,
the land is bright.

You looked for yourself
and all you found was other people.
You look for other people
and you end up with yourself again,
the land is bright.

When you've done
every doable poet on the block
the land is bright.

Holy shit! Some rich people
wear some bad clothes,
the land is bright.

You start to resent the tourists
not because they're here but
because they get to leave
and each new town is nothing but
repeats of all the towns
they passed through on the way,
the land is bright.

Today I told the truth
and others lied. Today I lied
while others spoke the truth.
The sun shone, clouds or no clouds, and
the land is bright.

Today some people took
numbers from the world and
others took those numbers and
made from them a different world
to better suit their paycheques
and still others showed us all
how to live in it as if we wanted to,
the land is bright.

It's the oldest trick:
don't just sell them a product,
sell them a way of life;
don't just sell them a way of life,
sell them an identity.
They're yours forever,
long as you can stop them finding out
WHAT I WANT IS NOT WHO I AM.

And when the crunch comes

it's the ones who can afford
to take the hit nearly always
turn out to be the ones
who can also afford not to have to,
the land is bright.

Listen, history being
just another writing exercise,
I have one for you.
I give you the opening lines,
rest of the poem is yours to finish:
use no words you wouldn't use,
say them just how you would say them
and here goes:

WELCOME TO THE UNITED REPUBLICS
OF THE ATLANTIC ARCHIPELAGO,
FORMERLY KNOWN BY SOME
AS THE BRITISH ISLES

ODES ONE ELEVEN

from the Latin of Horace

Don't you go bothering yourself, it's not our department, the
    endings the gods
have in store for me and for you, Martha my dear, and leave
    those bloody
horoscopes alone. Best you can, whatever it is, get on with it.
    There may be more winters,
this may be the last, seas crashing and rocks all obstinate.
    Now be a good girl,
open the wine; life is too small to let hopes grow untrimmed.
    Too much talk, the moment has
gone, fickle bastard. Today's the day. Don't rely too much on
    getting a sequel.

AFTER A COUPLET OF ROCHESTER

I hate all nations and the lies that underpin them,
from the French fucking Republic to the late United Kingdom.

THE DAY BEFORE THE CALENDAR RAN OUT

20th December 2012

Sheets of dirty rain gnaw
the colour from the streets.
The kitchen sink is choking.
My umbrella is too small.
I'm going to miss the bus and
tomorrow's the end of the world.

The windows of the phone shops,
every year the same tedious tinsel,
and the butcher's, with his pallid ranks
of turkeys, halal, of course, for that
traditional Muslim Christmas lunch
that nobody will eat because
tomorrow's the end of the world.

Up the retail districts
the deep glass canyons flood
with lights and things to buy in rivers.
Am I the only one with questions?
Where do these humans get the money?
Won't somebody talk holy to me?
Do black angels have white wings also?

The kitchen sink is choking.
My umbrella is too small.
I shouted at my sweetness and
tomorrow's the end of the world.

The blessed isles of history lie far upstream.
The pageant is done and this is the aftermath,
sandwich grease on serviettes, trampled
crowns of cardboard set with sugar jewels.
How long does the end of the world
usually take, anyway?

Will it be immediately blank, I wonder,
or howling to a small white dot?
Will they play the Mayan national anthem?
Or will the nights just not stop getting longer
as the timespring winds down?

The kitchen sink is choking up.
The fridge is full of bad leftovers.
My umbrella is too small.
Thieves abound at bus stations.
I shouted at my sweetness and
tomorrow's the end of the world.

FAGGOT HEXAMETERS

This is a poem about the first time someone called me a faggot.
Also, a poem that embroiders the truth a bit. Eighteen years old and
back in Newcastle for Christmas, having failed to get laid my whole
first term at college. Still jailbait, the age of consent being still twenty-
one and the tabloids and Tory grandees howling murderous triumph
over a dead generation of queer men, and warnings on local
news from your local vicar: the gays are after your children. They
actually used to broadcast that shit on Look North. Having left school, I
found myself drinking with sports-playing lads who would never have
looked at me short weeks before, in the kind of Neanderthal bar I'd
spent my whole drinking career so far keeping out of for safety.

Schooldays stopped feeling safe around twelve or thirteen. I don't like to
dwell on the grim masturbatory treadmill of male adolescence.
My first memories of sexual desire? Green shoots springing rotten
out of the soil, milk teeth with abscesses already in them, my
god, the shame hells of the steam-fogged changing rooms, where the wrong boy was
always the pasture your famished eyes were most desperate to graze. This
boy, for example: open-neck shirt, suggestion of chest hair,
fear of my schoolboy days and hero of many a sleepless
schoolboy night, no one used your arousal to keep you afraid quite
as deftly as this boy, this one at the bar, his attention distracted by
some passing pussy (his word, not mine). And, while we're on language, the

word we all knew for putting someone in his place was *gay*, for
marking him out or starting a fight or making him cry was
gay: the worst thing in the world you could be, even worse
    than a girl – whereas
faggot was alien, a word from the underground movies and JD
Salinger, four-colour sleaze and a world of alarm and adventure.
And, to be honest, where *gay* meant at best a high-functioning
    eunuch
kind of existence, *faggot* meant one day I might just get lucky.

Anyway, week before Christmas, back in the home town and
    this boy
finally sees who I am. 'Get that fucking faggot away from me!'
bursts on my head like a baptism. First time he's taken the
slightest notice of me in public, and I'm not about to
do anything that tears me away from those fearful, beautiful
eyes, and it's him drops his gaze, the way that I now know a
    lover
sometimes submits. The lads laugh and he leaves and I stay
    and the century
turned: we discovered the ones who were really after your
    children
were the respectable church-going types on the news,
    terrified, it
now becomes clear, that the gays would get to the sweet little
    morsels
first. Things get better: not everywhere, not without effort, but
    always;
even the Newcastle Arms has gone all leather sofas and lattes,
but that's a whole other poem, and this was a poem about
    when I
learned that it's not so much words as intentions. Still rather
    you call me
faggot than *gay*, to be frank, though I don't lose much sleep.
    In the world we all
want there'll be no need to specify, will there?

TWO LINES FROM HOMER

Humans grow the same way leaves do:
wind blows some to the ground,
the living wood grows more,
spring comes round again.

Same with us:
one human generation rises,
one generation falls away.

WE ARE POSTERITY

Once is a bit of fun, twice is a lot of fun,
three times is serious.

Shutting the eyes in the front of the head
opens the eyes in the back of it.

Poems without words, dancing to no music,
non-conversations in a bodily room.

Here, things that don't matter count the most:
one's hand is cold on the other's sweating neck;
sudden emptiness flowers, explodes and expires;
sweetness extends even to the ache it leaves behind.

This is the realest thing, our playground and our brothering.
What's the species to us, or us to the species?

We are posterity and we are unafraid,
at first because we don't know how it breaks the heart;
afterwards because we know it won't kill us.

TANTALOS

I search for the dark and find only light,
for death and nothing but resurrection.

Looking in only the lowest saloons for company,
I have no friends that aren't messiahs.

Hell must be somewhere
but everywhere is full of angels.

BRAVE NEW YEAR/HAPPY NEW WORLD

Elastic finally perishes, springs run dry, wind down.
So recently scintillating and now indigestible and flat
and blinking we emerge.

Dirt though, hands though, sooner or later
and I'm not even sure it was Kansas to begin with
and it certainly isn't now.

New Age bullshit aside, this is some time zone
in which to find ourselves. The poor kids are too fat,
the rich kids are too thin, the empire is over and
still that damn sun never sets.

One storyline peters out and we resolve that
there are always plenty more, with the risings of the tide
and the victories of days.

Once upon a time they say
hipsters were angel-headed,
sex and drugs, love and wine –
could we not skip the apocalypse
and just cut straight to the aftermath?

Tonite let's all make love in Luton
like it's a cold, wet Tuesday
and there's nothing on TV!

And we resolve that we always
looked like this; it's just that, in the dying years
of the last century, a conspiracy of poorer
and on the whole skinnier people
re-enacted key moments of our lives
in a series of photographs which they left behind them
when they disappeared, in the same brown envelope
as the handful of songs we didn't like at the time
and the ghosts of paperbacks we think we once owned.

O for a stiff salt breeze, sparse turf and scraggy clouds,
gulls, junk-shops and vans, a beautiful confusion
of chimneys, tops of trees and masts of sailing ships,
a fleet/a city/a forest, a place we've never been
and will none of us return!

O for the beat of a common heart,
the raising together of sweat
and drawing of loads, blood and breath
in harmony and work is a spree!

And we resolve that if it isn't rough
it won't polish.

And we resolve that we are all pigs
but some of us are learning how to fly.

ACKNOWLEDGEMENTS

This collection was originally to have been published by the late Gareth Lewis, to whose memory it is dedicated.

Thanks to all my families, poetic and otherwise, who helped one way or another to make this happen.

Particular love to Home Cooking (Newcastle), Utter! Spoken Word (London/Luton) and the PBH Spoken Word community at the Edinburgh Fringe; to fellow members of the Grandbaby Beat Generation (watch this space); last but not least to my husband Tim.